1

Table of Contents

The Author, Bill Rosoman Dip CS 2010

Introduction

Hi, Gidaye and Kia Ora.

This book grew out of my efforts to create ebooks in various formats to fit the various Ebook Readers like Kindle, Nook, Sony etc.

I acknowledge every bodies copyright etc. Personally I like copyleft or creative commons licences.

I particular acknowledge http://www.smashwords.com/ and http://www.lulu.com for some of the information and their excellent Publish On Demand (POD) websites.

My first real Ebook is at
http://www.smashwords.com/books/view/31925

An Ebook, EPUB, How To Write and Publish an Ebook, Using Free Software (FOSS), Writing and Publishing and Ebook is quite different from a Hard Copy Book.

This Ebook gives you all the Basic Software and Knowledge and Skills to Create Your Own Epics for the Modern Age.

Though nobody really knows where the digital publishing model is headed, Amazon already claim that they are selling more ebooks than traditional books. My good friend and associate Craig and I believe e-books are the way of the future and this will keep the "greenies" happy not having to cut down trees (see my article 'The Future of Electronic Publishing originally written about twelve years ago).

Software

I only use Free Software usually Free Open Source Software making Ebooks is the same.

I am using;

Kingsoft Office which looks and feels like Microsoft Office 2013 and is available free at http://www.kingsoftstore.com/download-office/index It is available in many formats unlike MS Office.

Open office To Type, Spell Check and Format Raw Text. http://www.openoffice.org

Calibre To Convert to EPUB Ebook to Test Document as an Ebook http://www.calibre-ebook.com

Google Chrome To Browse the Internet http://www.google.com/chrome

My OS is Linux Mint 17 (which is all Free) http://www.linuxmint.com/download.php

Foxit PDF Reader to Read PDF Files http://www.foxitsoftware.com/downloads/

The Gimp Graphics Editor for making a Front Cover

www.gimp.org

Inkscape Vector Graphics Editor

www.inkscape.org/download

All the Software is Free and Cross-platform, that is   it runs on Windows, Linux and Apple MAC and even Android Tablets/Smartphones.

We also extensively use the Cloud for Storing Stuff and even creating Documents and Slideshows in the Cloud.

We mainly use   https://drive.google.com   or https://onedrive.live.com/

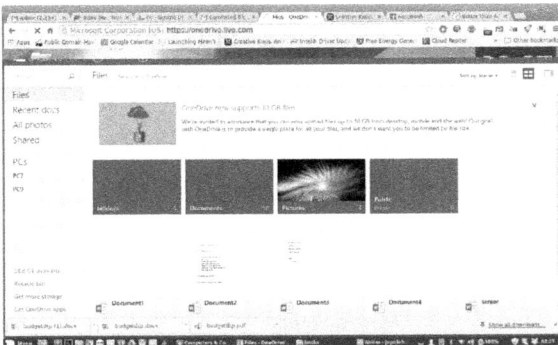

Some Interesting Websites

http://www.smashwords.com/ To Publish Ebooks and get Information

Amazon   Ebooks http://kdp.amazon.com/self-publishing/dashboard

To Publish a Printed Book on Amazon go to;

www.createspace.com

http://www.lulu.com To Publish Hard Copy Books and PDF Ebooks

My Websites:

Smashwords:

https://www.smashwords.com/profile/view/leftfieldnz

Main Website:

http://www.creativekiwis.com

Facebook:

http://www.facebook.com/leftfieldnz

Blog:

http://leftfieldnz.wordpress.com

How to Publish an Ebook on Amazon.com

I have found it quite easy to publish an Ebook on Amazon, but you have to remember that Amazon only supports their Kindle Ebook Reader. The next Chapter covers other formats at Smashwords.com.

Compose your book as normal in Kingsoft Office, Open Office, Libre Office or perhaps Microsoft Word.

Check the layout and create a Table of Contents.

If you want it perfect follow some of the style suggestions in the next Chapter on creating and Ebook on Smashwords.

On completion use Save As > Word Document (If you are not using MS Word).

To upload the Completed Ebook go to;
http://kdp.amazon.com/self-publishing/dashboard

Log in or Create and Account if you do not have one.

Add a New Title and follow the instructions and you are away.

You will need a cover graphic.

For help with creating an Amazon Ebook try;
https://kdp.amazon.com/self-publishing/help?icId=A17W8UM0MMSQX6

To Publish a Printed Book on Amazon go to;
www.createspace.com

Follow the normal procedures for creating a book.

The Nuts and Bolts of Writing an Ebook

This is mostly done in Kingsoft Office Writer or MS Office

Word.

The Easiest way is to follow the Smashwords style
Download their Style Guide at
http://www.smashwords.com/books/view/52

Smashwords are the Gold Standard, if you get Premium Status
with Smashwords, you have cracked most the formating, style,
layout problems.

Use Plain text using Default Paragraph Style IE Times New
Roman 11pt.
Do not use any fancy fonts or vary the size much. Certainly no
larger than 18 point.

If you are importing Text from another Document always Use
Edit > Paste Special > Paste as Unformatted Text. If this is not
available Use MS Notepad or Linux Kate or Gedit (Text
Editors) and then Select All (CTRL+A) Then Copy (CTRL+C).
Go to Ebook and Paste (CTRL+V).

Also use Images and Graphics sparingly as they will not
reproduce well in some Ebooks.
Make sure the images are Anchored and not Floating (Right
Click on an Image to Change to Anchor > As Character).
Now try Right Click Format Object > Layout > In line with
Text > OK.

For Chapter Add Bookmark
Highlight and Copy The Bookmark Name now Use Insert
Bookmark, Name the Bookmark with one word no spaces or

Paste the Name (CTRL+V) and Add

in the Table Of Contents at the front of the book add Hyperlink to the Bookmark

Use Insert > Hyperlink > Place in this Document > Paste Ctrl+V in Text to Display > Select Bookmark from the list > OK.

NB Have discovered that MS Word only likes One Word for Bookmarks and Hyperlinks. Open Office will use several words for a Bookmark.

Add   as a Bookmark in Table Of Contents and Hyperlink to it at the end of Chapters.

It is also good to make your Chapter Headings as TOC Heading One, it helps in setting the Bookmarks in a PDF version of the Ebook.

Format > Page > Page to Letter, as most books sold in USA if not use A4

Letter Size 216 mm x 279 mm or 8.5 x 11 inches

Now Highlight all the Text (CTRL+A) Use Format > Paragraph > Spacing and Indents > Spacing > Below Paragraph 0.06" > OK

Spell Check thoroughly and Check the Layout and Formatting. Turn on the Non-Printing Characters Tool on the Toolbar. You should only See this Character and Carriage Return   No TABS or Tables or Headers and

Footers or SPACE marks (Except between words) Etc. (Now under Writer/Word > Options > Paragraph Marks).

(From Style Guide at http://www.smashwords.com/books/view/52))

It's important you provide your readers visual cues to separate one paragraph from the next, otherwise paragraphs blend together and create a horrible reading experience. For the body of your book (everything after the title and copyright page), either use first line indents at the beginning of a paragraph, or use the block paragraph method. Don't use both.

Format Paragraph Indent

Use manual line feeds plus a paragraph return coded for a trailing "after" space. This option is a little more complicated, but will get you great results. To create a manual line feed, click Shift and Enter at the same time. A manual line feed creates a line break without invoking the styling of your paragraph style, which in the example below is coded for a trailing 10pt space after each paragraph return. Note how only the question and the last answer have their lines terminated with a paragraph return (created by hitting the Enter key). Use this trick for poetry as well.

At the Beginning of the book you add
Smashwords Edition

This ebook is licensed for your personal enjoyment only.

This ebook may not be re-sold or given away to other people. If you would like to share this book with another person, please purchase an additional copy for each recipient. If you're reading this book and did not purchase it, or it was not purchased for your use only, then please return to https://www.smashwords.com/profile/view/leftfieldnz and purchase your own copy. Thank you for respecting the hard work of this author.

As well book title, author etc.

At the end of the book put the following
###

To test the Book Use File > Export as PDF > OK
Locate the File and Open with Foxit Reader or Adobe Reader.
Check the Links and Layout and Formatting.

To test the EPUB Book Use File > Save As > Select PDF > Name the File
Open the PDF File with Calibre an then convert to an EPUB Ebook

BTW Just discovered you need to change the file information, go to Writer/Word > File Information > Properties, and edit the information.

Publish an Ebook on lulu.com

Www.lulu.com have now separated their printed books and

ebooks.

Go to lulu, log in and create and Ebook.

Go to MY Lulu
Start a New Project
Select Ebook
Follow the Instructions and you will see be published online.

Lulu ebooks are quite difficult. If you upload a PDF file you can publish your Ebook on Lulu quite quick and easy.

If you wish to have other formats of Ebooks upload as a EPUB or Doc, but I have found this just too hard and Smashwords does a similar thing anyway.

So I just upload the PDF for an Ebook on Lulu

Another way to create a PDF file is to upload it to www.zamzar.com and then convert a .doc or .docx.

Create a Cover Graphic

I use Open Office Draw, Inkscape and The Gimp to create a front cover.

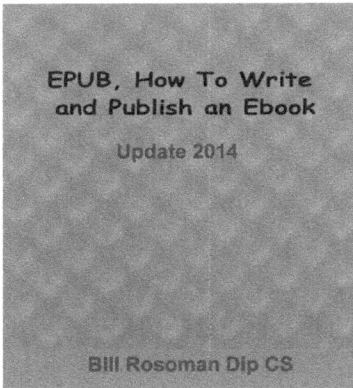

I have found with Createspace it can be easier use one of there covers.

For Smashwords needs to be 1200 by 1400 pixels.

Using Calibre

Convert to EPUB to Test Your Creation.

Create a TXT or ODT Document as above, Use File > Save As > Select PDF > OK

Open Calibre

Add Book you have created

Highlight Your New Book, Press Convert E-Books

Select Output format on first page   Right as EPUB

Change Cover Image to one You have Created.

Add Title > Author > Publisher > Comments

Press OK

When Conversion Finished Press View.

Make sure to Check the Layout and All The Links.

Calibre supports the conversion of many input formats to many output formats. It can convert every input format in the following list, to every output format.

Input Formats: CBZ, CBR, CBC, CHM, EPUB, FB2, HTML, LIT, LRF, MOBI, ODT, PDF, PRC**, PDB, PML, RB, RTF, SNB, TCR, TXT

Output Formats: EPUB, FB2, OEB, LIT, LRF, MOBI, PDB, PML, RB, PDF, SNB, TCR, TXT

** PRC is a generic format, calibre supports PRC files with TextRead and MOBIBook headers

What are the best source formats to convert?

Upload and Publish Ebook

Once Tested and Corrected you Need to Save As a Word Document.

Use File > Save As > Select Word Document > Name File and Save

BTW The source file you upload must be smaller than 5 megabytes. If it is larger you may have to reduced the size of the pictures you are using.

Now you just need to Signup and Logon to Smashwords
http://www.smashwords.com/

And Press Publish, Fill out the Form and Publish.

Smashwords will Convert to Ebook and let you know if it is successful.

My First one passed with Flying Colours so it is not too hard LOL.

Upload manuscripts in Microsoft Word .doc format.

Or, if your file is already prepared in an ebook format, you may upload:

epub (.epub)

(Maximum file size: 10MB.)

If you need to Convert Between Formats IE PDF to DOC Try

http://www.zamzar.com/

Other Information

(From   Style   Guide   at
http://www.smashwords.com/books/view/52)

Open Office users only: Open Office users often have trouble with images, because OO defaults to floating. If you're an Open Office user, try entering a paragraph return on a blank line where you want the image to appear, and then   click in front of the paragraph return and go to Insert: Picture: From File, then select the image to import it, then right mouse click on the image in Open Office, then select Anchor: As Character, then click your mouse to the right of the image, then click OO's center button to center the image

Naming Your Chapters: If you name your chapters starting with the word "Chapter," Meatgrinder (the Smashwords Converter) will automatically detect the word and build useful navigation links into your EPUB file.

Here's what your TOC might look like:

Table of Contents

Chapter 1 – The Beginning

Chapter 2 – The Middle

Chapter 3 – More in the Middle

Chapter 4 – The Final Chapter

Etc.

You can left-justify it (as I did above) or center it using Word's center button. Never indent your TOC more than one inch.

Smashwords Formats:

(From   Style   Guide   at http://www.smashwords.com/books/view/52)

EPUB - This is your most important format! EPUB is an open industry ebook format. This is the format Smashwords distribute to Apple, Barnes&Noble, Sony, Kobo, Diesel eBooks, and others. If your book is available in epub, it can be read on the most popular ebook readers and ebook reading software applications (Like Stanza on the iPhone or Aldiko on Android devices), and will gain the widest distribution via Smashwords' distribution outlets (EPUB is a requirement for inclusion in

Smashwords' Premium Catalog, and it's what Smashwords distribute to every retailer except Amazon).

Mobipocket (Kindle) – Mobipocket, A.K.A. MOBI, allows your books to be read on the

Amazon Kindle, so this is an important format for you. Mobipocket is supported on many

handheld devices and e-reading applications. Mobipocket is a requirement for distribution to Amazon.

Palm Doc (PDB) - PalmDoc is a format primarily used on Palm Pilot devices, but software readers are available for PalmOS, Symbian OS, Windows Mobile Pocket PC/Smartphone, desk Windows, and Macintosh. Be sure to turn off "smart quotes" in your source file, otherwise they may appear garbled in your PDB file. Our PDB is little more than ugly plain text.

PDF - Portable Document Format, or PDF, is a file format readable by most devices, including handheld e-readers, PDAs, and personal computers. It's a good format if your work contains complex layout, charts or images. Odds are, if your work looks good in Microsoft Word it will look good in PDF. PDF is also a good option for readers who may want to print out your book on their home computers. On the negative side, PDF is a rigid, inflexible format because it's not reflowable, so it's horrible for reading novels. Your customers can't easily change the font size or style to match their preferences, the text isn't reflowable, and the reader is forced to read page by page.

LRF - This is the old format for the Sony Reader. Sony has shifted to the EPUB format, so LRF is less important than it once was.

RTF - Rich Text Format, or RTF, is a cross-platform document format supported by many word processors and devices. It's usually pretty good at preserving the original formatting from Word documents.

Plain Text - Plain text is the most widely supported file format. It works on nearly all readers and devices. It lacks formatting, but will work anywhere. For best results with plain text, your source document should not contain images or fancy formatting.

HTML SmashReader – This is our online reader that allows customers to sample or read your book from their web browser. Your sample pages will be indexed by Google, which will increase the ability for potential customers to find your book, even if they didn't know your book is what they were looking for. Think of it as serendipity on steroids. If your book looks good in our

HTML reader, it will probably also look good in EPUB and MOBI. Linked tables of contents (TOC'S) don't work in the HTML reader.

Javascript SmashReader - This online reader isn't indexable by search engines like the HTML reader, but it does allow your readers to customize their reading experience. They can increase or decrease the fonts, change the line spacing, change the font, change the font colour or the background colour. Our Javascript Reader has always been a bit buggy, so if you see strange characters along the   of the page, ignore them. Linked TOC'S don't work here.

ISBN Numbers

You need one ISBN Number for each book and each format.

https://www.smashwords.com/dashboard/ISBNManager

Obtain an ISBN number

Now your ebook is taking shape we need to sharpen our pencil and get organised so we can get the ebook published and up and out there!

So the first thing we have to do is get an ISBN number.

An ISBN number is the Books unique International number. You can not publish an ebook without one effectively!

In New Zealand ISBN numbers are controlled by the NZ National Library and can be obtained from

http://www.natlib.govt.nz/services/get-advice/publishing/isbn/isbn-application

Email ISBN@natlib.govt.nz

Overseas there is places like

www.isbn.org

or www.smashwords.com will sell you an ISBN Number.

PS I have been given a batch of 100 ISBN numbers to allocate to the ebooks I am writing and publishing.

You need ten ISBN for each ebook format, as there are nine ebook formats and one for a printed book. Hmm just had a look and Smashwords require one ISBN for Ebook and a separate one if you do a printed book. My advice is really you need an ISBN for each format of your ebook.

Smashwords has an ISBN Manger at http://www.smashwords.com/dashboard/ISBNManager this gives you all the information on ISBN Numbers.

USA Tax on Book/Ebook Sales

If you are a non resident of the USA IE an Alien, then you will be taxed at 30% for sales on USA resident sites like Amazon, Lulu and Smashwords.

Some Countries like New Zealand have a reciprocal tax treaty with the USA.

You can therefore with a lot of red tape get an exemption and pay a lot less tax.

I estimate for me to do will cost around $US150.

So you would have to way up the number of potential sales with the amount of tax you will pay.

You need

IRS Form W-7 Application for IRS Individual Taxpayer Identification Number

www.irs.gov/w7

An IRS individual taxpayer identification number (ITIN) is for federal tax purposes only.

IRS Form W-8BEN Certificate of Foreign Status of Beneficial Owner for United States Withholding

These publications are available free from the IRS. To order the publications, call 1-800-TAX-FORM (1-800-829-3676) if you are in the United States. If you have a foreign address, write to:

Internal Revenue Service

1201 N. Mitsubishi Motorway

Bloomington, IL 61705-6613

You also can get these publications at www.irs.gov/formspubs

Telephone help. If, after reading these instructions and our free publications, you are not sure how to complete your application or have additional questions, call 1-800-829-1040 if you are in the United States, call 267-941-1000 (not a toll-free number) or contact our originates in a country that is nct party to the Convention, overseas offices in Beijing, Frankfurt, London, or Paris.

You also need to have several forms of ID. See the documentation.

Some documents you have to have Sent for Authentication or Apostille of Documents in your local country.

In New Zealand it is Internal Affairs Authentication Unit Phone: +64 4 470 2928 (if overseas) Freephone: 0800 872 675 (NZ only) Fax: +64 4 470 2921 Email: authentication@egs.govt.nz

Send to:
By post OR
Authentication Unit
PO Box 805
Wellington 6140
New Zealand

By courier/in person
Authentication Unit
Level 13, Prime Property Tower
86-90 Lambton Quay
Wellington 6011
New Zealand

Final Thoughts

I have spent many hours researching and compiling these ebooks. I have learnt a lot about different Word Processor Software and about layout etc.

It is easy enough to create and ebook and get it accepted. The trick is to get the format and layout right so your ebook is accepted for the Smashwords Premium Distribution. That is were you will get far better sales,

Getting an ebook accepted into the Smashwords Premium Distribution has proved to be quite a learning curve and mission.

But that is part of life, Smashwords have to meet the best standards and the standards of those they provide content to like Amazon.

Best of Luck!

Bill Rosoman Books/Ebooks

The Ultimate Desk Publishing Book

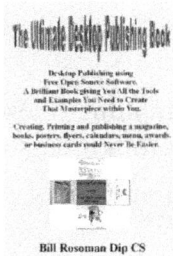

Desk Publishing using Free Open Source Software. A Brilliant Book giving You All the Tools and Examples You Need to Create That Masterpiece within You. Creating and publishing a magazine, books, posters, flyers, calendar, menu, award certificates, or business cards could Never Be Easier. Using Free Open Source Software FOSS. Scribus, Open Office, Gimp, Inkscape, Calibre. By Bill Rosoman Dip CS

http://www.lulu.com/product/paperback/the-ultimate-desk-publishing-book/14847923

Android Tablet Apads How to

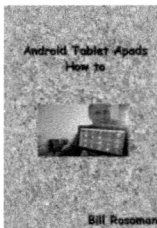

Android Tablets Apad How to", Some great Information for the use of Android Tablets. Tablets are the device of the future.

http://www.smashwords.com/books/view/35819

Puppy Linux Manual

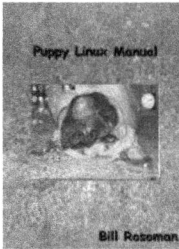

An ebook, "Puppy Linux Manual", Some great Information for the use of Puppy Linux, a Free Operating System which is great on older computers. Puppy Linux is also good for formatting and partitioning hard drives and rescuing data from crash computers.

http://www.smashwords.com/books/view/35818

Creative Kiwis, an Amazing Journey

Bill Rosoman and Craig Lock

An ebook, "Creative Kiwis, an Amazing Journey", this book is about the journey of two people in the world of the Internet and Ebook and Book Publishing and Marketing. A massive journey and learning process.

http://www.smashwords.com/books/view/43270

Creative Kiwis an Amazing Journey.

We have many Books and Ebooks Available for your enjoyment and enlightenment.

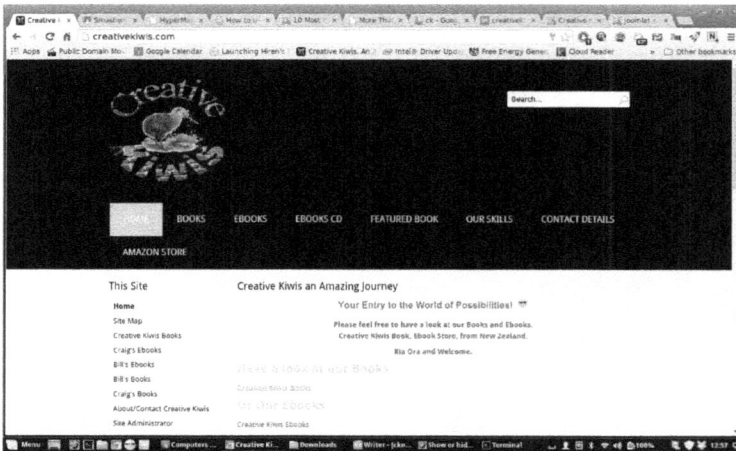

www.creativekiwis.com

About Creative Kiwis

www.creativekiwis.com is a joint venture between Craig and Bill.

Creative Kiwis is our Empire, our Portal to the World.

It provides us with a Platform to Promote mostly our Books and Ebooks.

It has been a fantastic journey of discovery and enlightenment.

Bills Bio

Bill Rosoman's Dip CS Skills

Bill has;

a Diploma in Computing stream Support, Level five

30 years computer experience

a passion for computing, telecommunications and the internet

been an author and publisher for many years

been a successful Book/Ebook Publisher on

http://www.smashwords.com/profile/view/leftfieldnz

http://www.lulu.com/spotlight/leftfieldnz

http://www.amazon.com/s/ref=nb_sb_noss?url=search-alias%3
Daps&field-keywords=%22bill+rosoman%22

been specialising in doing book layout, book covers and getting the books and ebooks published online and selling

If Bill can help you get your Book or Ebook Online or if you need a Website or similar contact him now

leftfieldnz@gmail.com

Craigs Bio

Craig Lock's BA Skills

Craig has;

a BA

Spent many years in the corporate world in South Africa and New Zealand. Financial Services.

written some brochures on Money Management

been an author and publisher for many years

been a successful Book/Ebook Publisher on

Amazon http://goo.gl/8Xawh

http://www.smashwords.com/profile/view/craiglock

Lulu http://goo.gl/M2GbM

many years experience with internet promotion and marketing

many years experience in proof reading books

If Craig can help get your project off the ground contact him now

craiglock@xtra.co.nz

Creative Kiwis, an Amazing Journey.

Books, Ebooks, Audio Books and much more

www.creativekiwis.com

Bill Rosoman ebooks on Smashwords

http://www.smashwords.com/profile/view/leftfieldnz

Bill Rosoman books and ebooks on Lulu.com

http://stores.lulu.com/leftfieldnz

Bill Rosoman Amazon.com books/ebooks

http://goo.gl/MLSLL

Craig Lock Amazon.com books/ebooks

http://goo.gl/vTpjk

Craig Lock ebooks on Smashwords

https://www.smashwords.com/profile/view/craiglock

Craig Lock books and ebooks on Lulu.com

http://www.lulu.com/spotlight/craiglock

Creative Kiwis Videos at

www.youtube.com/leftfieldnz

Creative Kiwis Blog

http://leftfieldnz.wordpress.com/

An ebook, "EPUB, How To Write and Publish an Ebook", using free software (FOSS), Writing and publishing and ebook is quite different from a hard copy book. This ebook gives you all the basic software and knowledge and skills to create your own epics for the modern age.

Keywords: EPUB, Ebooks, Publishing, Print On Demand, Publish, Write Ebook, Free Software, Writing, Books. FOSS, Free Open Source Software

###